AMERICAN PRESIDENTS

Ronald Reagan

by Rachel Grack

BELLWETHER MEDIA • MINNEAPOLIS, MN

Blastoff! Readers are carefully developed by literacy experts to build reading stamina and move students toward fluency by combining standards-based content with developmentally appropriate text.

Level 1 provides the most support through repetition of high-frequency words, light text, predictable sentence patterns, and strong visual support.

Level 2 offers early readers a bit more challenge through varied sentences, increased text load, and text-supportive special features.

Level 3 advances early-fluent readers toward fluency through increased text load, less reliance on photos, advancing concepts, longer sentences, and more complex special features.

★ **Blastoff! Universe**

Reading Level

Grade **K**

Grades **1–3**

Grade **4**

This edition first published in 2022 by Bellwether Media, Inc.

No part of this publication may be reproduced in whole or in part without written permission of the publisher. For information regarding permission, write to Bellwether Media, Inc., Attention: Permissions Department, 6012 Blue Circle Drive, Minnetonka, MN 55343.

Library of Congress Cataloging-in-Publication Data

Names: Koestler-Grack, Rachel A., 1973- author.
Title: Ronald Reagan / by Rachel Grack.
Description: Minneapolis, MN : Bellwether Media, 2022. | Series: Blastoff! Readers: American Presidents | Includes bibliographical references and index. | Audience: Ages 5-8 | Audience: Grades 2-3 | Summary: "Relevant images match informative text in this introduction to Ronald Reagan. Intended for students in kindergarten through third grade"-- Provided by publisher.
Identifiers: LCCN 2021011415 (print) | LCCN 2021011416 (ebook) | ISBN 9781644875186 (library binding) | ISBN 9781648344862 (paperback) | ISBN 9781648344268 (ebook)
Subjects: LCSH: Reagan, Ronald--Juvenile literature. | United States--Politics and government--1981-1989--Juvenile literature. | Presidents--United States--Biography--Juvenile literature.
Classification: LCC E877 .K64 2022 (print) | LCC E877 (ebook) | DDC 973.927092--dc23
LC record available at https://lccn.loc.gov/2021011415
LC ebook record available at https://lccn.loc.gov/2021011416

Text copyright © 2022 by Bellwether Media, Inc. BLASTOFF! READERS and associated logos are trademarks and/or registered trademarks of Bellwether Media, Inc.

Editor: Elizabeth Neuenfeldt   Designer: Josh Brink

Printed in the United States of America, North Mankato, MN.

Table of Contents

Who Was Ronald   4
Reagan?

Time in Office   12

What Ronald Left   20
Behind

Glossary   22

To Learn More   23

Index   24

Who Was Ronald Reagan?

Ronald Reagan was the 40th president. He led the United States from 1981 to 1989.

He helped end the **Cold War**.

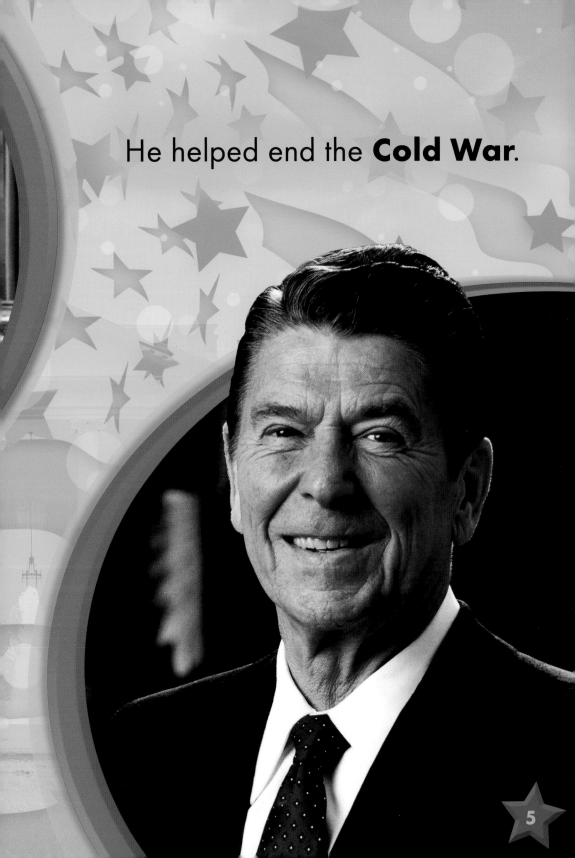

Ronald's Hometown

Tampico, Illinois

Dixon, Illinois

N W E S

Ronald was born in Tampico, Illinois, in 1911. He grew up in Dixon.

He loved playing sports.
He also spent summers as
a **lifeguard**.

In 1928, Ronald went to Eureka College. He was student president!

Presidential Picks

Books

The Hunt for Red October and *The Bible*

Sports

swimming, golf, and football

Food

jelly beans

Movie

The Sound of Music

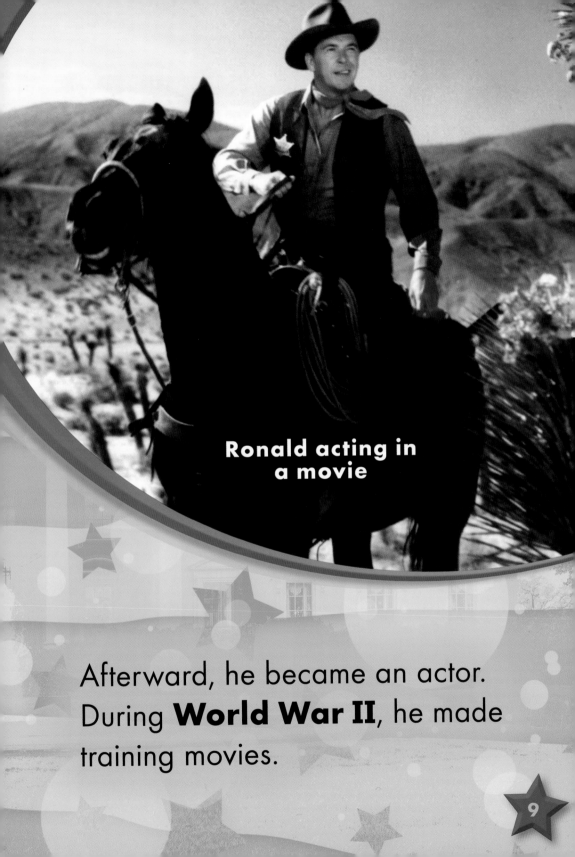

**Ronald acting in
a movie**

Afterward, he became an actor.
During **World War II**, he made
training movies.

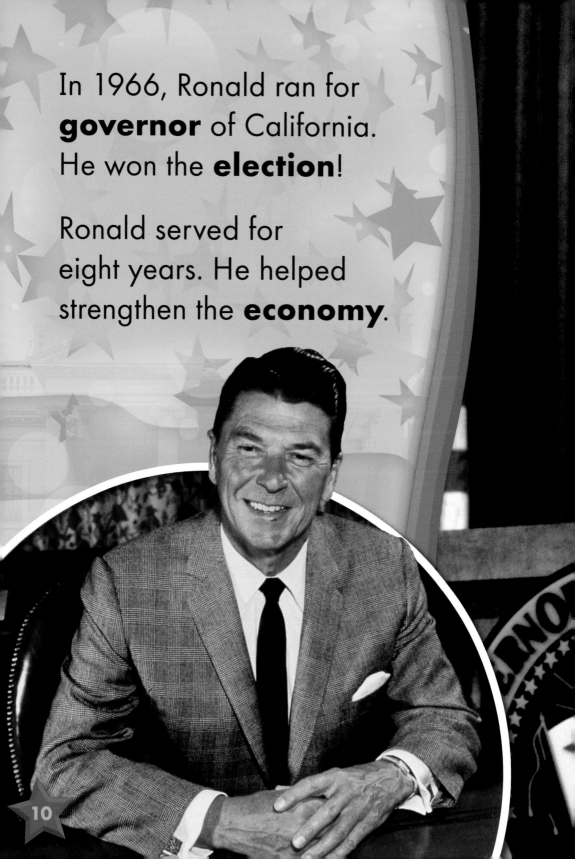

In 1966, Ronald ran for **governor** of California. He won the **election**!

Ronald served for eight years. He helped strengthen the **economy**.

Question

What helped Ronald become president?

Ronald was elected president in 1980. He was **inaugurated** in January 1981.

On March 30, he was shot in Washington, D.C. But he lived! Soon, he returned to office.

Presidential Profile

Place of Birth

Tampico, Illinois

Birthday

February 6, 1911

Schooling

Eureka College

Term

1981 to 1989

Party

 Republican

Signature

Ronald Reagan

Vice President

George H. W. Bush

Ronald led during the Cold War. He spoke out against the **Soviet Union**.

He wanted to keep the U.S. safe.
He strengthened the military.

Ronald wanted to help the economy. He cut **taxes** for people and businesses. He hoped this would help businesses grow.

Ronald Timeline

1980

Ronald Reagan is elected president

March 30, 1981

Ronald is shot in Washington, D.C.

1981

Ronald begins plans to strengthen the military

1984

Ronald is reelected

December 8, 1987

Ronald and Soviet leaders sign a treaty

1988

Ronald visits the Soviet Union

January 20, 1989

Ronald leaves office

1991

The Cold War ends

Ronald was reelected in 1984. He worked for peace with Soviet leaders.

Ronald with the leader of the Soviet Union

In 1987, he signed a **treaty** with them. He later visited the Soviet Union.

Ronald's work made way for peace. The Cold War ended in 1991.

In 2004, Ronald died.
He is remembered for his
strong leadership!

Glossary

Cold War—the conflict between the U.S. and the Soviet Union in the second half of the 1900s that did not break out into fighting

economy—the way a state or country makes, sells, and uses goods and services

election—an event in which people vote to choose leaders

governor—the leader of the government of a state

inaugurated—sworn into public office

lifeguard—someone trained to save swimmers in danger

Soviet Union—a former country in eastern Europe and western Asia that lasted lasted from 1922 to 1991

taxes—money paid to the government that is used for public projects

treaty—an agreement between two or more countries

World War II—the war fought from 1939 to 1945 that involved many countries

To Learn More

AT THE LIBRARY

Britton, Tamara L. *Ronald Reagan.* Minneapolis, Minn.:
Abdo Publishing, 2020.

Messner, Kate. *The Next President: The Unexpected
Beginnings and Unwritten Future of America's Presidents.*
San Francisco, Calif.: Chronicle Books, 2020.

Rustad, Martha E. H. *The President of the United States.*
North Mankato, Minn.: Pebble, 2020.

ON THE WEB

FACTSURFER

Factsurfer.com gives you
a safe, fun way to find
more information.

1. Go to www.factsurfer.com.

2. Enter "Ronald Reagan" into the search box
   and click 🔍.

3. Select your book cover to see a list
   of related content.

Index

actor, 9

businesses, 16

California, 10

Cold War, 5, 14, 20

Dixon, Illinois, 6

economy, 10, 16

election, 10, 12, 18

Eureka College, 8

governor, 10

hometown, 6

inaugurated, 12

leadership, 4, 14, 21

lifeguard, 7

military, 15

movies, 9

peace, 18, 20

picks, 8

profile, 13

question, 11

Soviet Union, 14, 18, 19

sports, 7

student president, 8

Tampico, Illinois, 6

taxes, 16

timeline, 17

treaty, 19

Washington, D.C., 13

World War II, 9

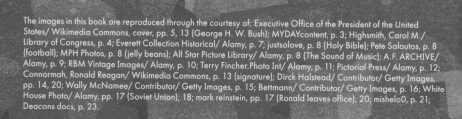

The images in this book are reproduced through the courtesy of: Executive Office of the President of the United States/ Wikimedia Commons, cover, pp. 5, 13 (George H. W. Bush); MYDAYcontent, p. 3; Highsmith, Carol M./ Library of Congress, p. 4; Everett Collection Historical/ Alamy, p. 7; justsolove, p. 8 (Holy Bible); Pete Saloutos, p. 8 (football); MPH Photos, p. 8 (jelly beans); All Star Picture Library/ Alamy, p. 8 (The Sound of Music); A.F. ARCHIVE/ Alamy, p. 9; RBM Vintage Images/ Alamy, p. 10; Terry Fincher.Photo Int/ Alamy, p. 11; Pictorial Press/ Alamy, p. 12; Connormah, Ronald Reagan/ Wikimedia Commons, p. 13 (signature); Dirck Halstead/ Contributor/ Getty Images, pp. 14, 20; Wally McNamee/ Contributor/ Getty Images, p. 15; Bettmann/ Contributor/ Getty Images, p. 16; White House Photo/ Alamy, pp. 17 (Soviet Union); 18; mark reinstein, pp. 17 (Ronald leaves office), 20; mishelo0, p. 21; Deacons docs, p. 23.